EASING THE

Collected Poems

J.G. Jolly

Published by Palores Publications 2010

Easing The Burden
Edited & Compiled S. Jolly 2010
Copyright © S. Jolly 2010

Front Cover:
Copyright © S. Jolly 2010
Front cover photograph of Nanpean United Methodist Chapel,
St. Stephen-in-Brannel by kind permission of Mr. David Thomas.

ISBN No 978-1-906845-09-4

Published by:
Palores Publications,
I I a Penryn Street,
Redruth,
Cornwall.
TR15 2SP

Designed and printed by:
ImageSet,
63 Tehidy Road,
Camborne,
Cornwall.
TR10 8LJ

Typeset in:
Sabon 12/14

BIOGRAPHY

Jack Jolly 1920-2003

My Father *Jack* John Jolly was born in 1920 in Stithians, Cornwall in a cottage , which he always maintained, now lies under the waters of Stithians Dam. He was brought up in the nearby village of Lanner , with a younger brother and sister by their recently widowed Mother. These were hard days for Cornwall, and with little hope of gaining local employment my Father joined The Devon and Cornwall Light Infantry in 1938. And was sent straight out to India, where he stayed till after the end of the Second World War. The contrast between India in the dying days of the British Empire and my Fathers traditional chapel going, Bible reading childhood must have been startling. This culture shock gave him, I believe the initial spark for and continuing desire to write, which really blossomed on his eventual return to Cornwall in 1960.

Sarah Jolly
2009

Acknowledgements

Poetry
Thanks are due to the Editors of the following magazines, journals, radio programmes and Gorseth Kernow competitions in which some of these poems have been first printed, awarded or heard:

The Cornish Review in 1967, 1968 1972 and 1973
The South West Review 1977
Cornish Dialect and English Verse featured on BBC1s'
'The South Bank Show' and BBC 2s' 'Second House'
John Harry Society Newsletter

Winner of the Gorseth Kernow Poetry Competition for English and Cornish Dialect Verse between 1969 and 1974 and Highly Commended in 1973.

Contents

EASING THE BURDEN

When I bemoan my lot
Don't bother overmuch —
I'll do with what I've got.

(I'm short on juggernauting ambition;
I'm missing genes of acquisition-
The buddles that separate rich pay sand
From endless streams of low-grade tailings.)

Just give some time to those
Who pray for Queens and Kings
And Ministers, and Things.
Who love the status quo
Because it suits them so.

And, then, there are the poor; the sick;
The old who wait outside your gate,
And, God knows (beg pardon), all those
Who don't bemoan their piteous state.

Buddles - Devise to remove tin from sand and water.

THE MONEY BIRD

Am I cuckold without culture
That I'm Father to a fowl as
Ugly as a Pterodactyl
Greedy as an empty vulture.

Slaving for this evil chicken
Robs me of my faith in Human
Nature, gobbles up my dreams, and
Now my heart with fear is stricken.

Fears that whine and nag and chivvy
Tell me that bird will doubtless
Claim my life and leave me pennies
Two – to which I'll not be privy.

CORNISH SEASONS

Sewrah Spring

The domino – ludo – 'Robinson Crusoe' –
Magic lantern evenings all but gone.
Day long the sprung-wool lambs played pogo-stick
With gravity where grassy fields slope down
To the millstream's edge. There laid-up trees,
Stood out at last their great green sails unfurled,
Their topmost pennants waving tauntingly.
Tempted thus we climbed and sailed our days away.
And watched the sturdy carts, so far below,
Go lumbering, heavy laden, from the mill
Along lanes to Hendra,Gear, Tregolls
Treweege,Trewithen or to Tubbon Hill.
And caught the fitful glint of polished brass
As sweating shires strained at their loads between
Sweet smelling hedgerows on those ways that lead,
Beyond our youthful horizons, to strange lands,
Deserts, jungles , and deep seas where the wind
Does not stir the cabined country boys who sailed,
In Springtime, above Sewrahs' green fields.

CORNISH SEASONS

Gonorman High Summer

Above the grass about my face
Fat bees bumble by on humdrum
Flights from flower to flower
To shady hedge and back again;
Somewhere over byTrevales
In a sun-steeped field
A cow lows plaintively;
Down by the Kennal, its whistle piping clear,
A little train is chundling slowly
On towards some distant Never-Never Land;
A bold skylark starts to build
A slender shaft of golden sound
Against the brassy sky –
Then shaft and bird are gone
And all is – sleepy – still;
With seductive grace a Painted Lady
Teeters out of sight
Down invisible corridors of air.
My head sinks lower in the sweet, warm grass,
And for a slumberous while I no longer
Stumble drunkenly along the tortuous
Passages of love.

CORNISH SEASONS

Kennal Valley Autumn

The stiff brambles veining the fading undergrowth
Makes progress slower than did
The suppler stems of spring.
These paths, once well trod
By strong and tolerant men who wrested
The hard, grey heart from this tight valley,
Are returning now to natures' anonymity.
Looking in the dark, deep quarry-lake.
Golden fleeced with autumn leaves,
I clearly see a pit with swirling dust
Enshrouding all who laboured there and lingering
With selected hosts to prove a mortal kinship.
I recalled the sounds of yesterday –
Rattle of chain and skep;
Clink of hammered anvil;
Rasp, rasp of shot fed saws;
Spattering of blasted chippings falling through the leafy trees.
I wondered how my daughter, city bred,
Felt in this place where once blood of her blood
Pulsed to the thumping hammer and ringing drill.
She saw, across the still water,
A kestrel perched – wings outspread – embossed
Upon the massive granite face those rose beneath
Crown of ash, sycamore and beech,
Embellished by a fruiting rowan tree.
She could not know that this made.
A memorial befitting, in its magnificence,
To all who laboured there.
From the autumn trees fell bright remembrances.

CORNISH SEASONS

Tretheague Winter

Now are the cassette-recorder,hi-fi stereo,
'Clockwork Orange', television days
When my daughter dances, zombie like, or sits
Entranced by some eldritch,yelping'star'.
Small birds perch crumpt against a cutting wind
That knifes across the fields and moor;
Overhead the sea gale truant gulls
Gyre, twist, and screech across the slatey sky.
I see the first snowfall of winter edge
Bald fields about Tregonning and Tregolls,
And wonder if on such a day as this
A lonely preaching man found haven here
Beneath the wild percussion of the trees.
For such there must have been because a Cross
That by the farmyard gate stands, bears silent witness
To the Church that came to a dark land
Where magic of the oak and mistletoe
Reigned supreme, and preached the Mystery
And of the Great Renewal.

QUARTET

JOHN HARRIS

To-day he goes down with me – rung
By rung, length on length, down to
The sulphurous entrails of the earth.
Through gutted aisles to stoped cathedrals
Where, by fitful candlelight,
Mammon holds his bestial rites
Choosing sacrificial lambs at random.
John's little boots their purchase
Make rung by rung – lest he tires
Before the darkest depths are reached
I'll let him on my shoulders sit,
And we'll go down as one – rung by rung
I'll not see the fear crawl o'er his face
As sun gives way to stars – unnatural night.
Lord, for this pittance must he go
Who, snug in Bolenoe bowers,
Watched the sunshine showers thread stars
Along the stems of swaying flowers ?

QUARTET

PETER LANYON

Sometimes a vagrant wind blows'
Aside the grass that guards
The small broken frame; the skeletal wings
With their vestigial covering;
The navigator's bared dome
From where once there came
Precise instructions that held it
Hovering, sent it diving, spinning.
Gliding, soaring – so high that Gunnards Head,
Godrevy Light, St. Michael's Mount
Seemed but static specks along a spinning track.
Sometimes the manbird artist joined it there,
And looking down the thermal kaleidoscope
Saw that which he would lovingly record –
Sometimes a vagrant wind blows.

QUARTET

NEVILLE NORTHEY BURNARD

W'en I go down Church Laane, behind th' Scala,
An' theer's a ayst'ly wend blawen' 'ard,
I thenk ov that ol' tramp en theer – ovver th' wall
En ower churchyard – all th' way
From Lundun tu 'is last spike.
'e wus rite faamus up theer they say,
At skulpteren', or drawen', 'e 'rld kwite a sway.
Sumthe' went wrong – booze I'll lay odds-
Chucked et all an' tuk tu th' Keng's 'ighway.
Went up frum Alternun wen but a booy,
An' cum a brawken ol' man–
A ayst'ly krewl up theer on th' moor
Wen yur sexty, brawk-up, an starven' poor.
'e'd lost sumthen' or other, I've 'erd,
An' en' is searchen' 'ad got as fur as Redruth –
'e wus pecked up fut ded frum a keddley floor
An' karted off tu th' werk'owse where, at last,
Th' dayp skrowled slate wus wiped klane
As th' plane stawn en theer marken 'es graver.

9

QUARTET

JACK CLEMO

The clay –
Chosen without apparent heed
To quality or condition –
The Potter threw onto the spinning wheel.
He smiled –
That inscrutable smile –
He knew from what harsh firing would come forth
A vessel full worthy of its use.

The Lord chose him
He placed His hands upon him
The Lord blessed him with darkness.
The Lord chose him
And, in the silent darkness, shaped him.

Great is the joy of the Elect
Beautiful the songs he sings.

JUST THIS ONCE

**(For Jack Clemo on
his Wedding Day)**

Come, dear poet, just his once
Let rails be ropes
To swing the clay dune bells
In carillon above moorland slopes.

And let the clapper Skeps give tongues
To our great joy
For once whose fierce, pure faith
Finds truth and strength in Life's cruel Calvary.

Come, dear poet, just this once
Let Mammon's scars
Be swept away and there
Be only candled gorse to guide the stars.

And with the dawn no cold dune arcs
To glare the rings
Where piskies danced all night
To celebrate true love's sweet victory.

BANISHED TO THE WESTERN HILLS
(For Charles Causley)

In an evil pique my Lord sent me
From my post by the busy Ham
To these barren, windswept Western Hills:
Unhappy exile trapt behind grey castle walls.

The clock in the hall drips slowly,
At the door my sandals lie unused
The lonely paths rarely feel their tread:
There I meet familiars of distant friends.

Coiling mists crawl over the stepped hills.
Over the Willow Garden, dragging black Winter's
Frozen Wheel slowly into the darkening sky
To glare balefully on my dreams.

I would leave this land of stone-skinners
And happily return to my old haunts:
To the sound of flute and flageolet:
To the lilting laughter of dancing girls.

Back to the warmth of old friends
And rich wines – here the harp unplayed,
Drinking an unfriendly wine- wondering how he
Sings so happily so far from the sea.

CLOSE-UP
of S.B.D - 1885-1978

1885 –
Waiting for the baby to be born
In mirage oasis
Where serpents are.

Fearing that despairing, urgent cry
For the orchids in the tree
Where the leopards lurk.

Playing as a child for so few years –
Then the chattering machine
Conned her childhood away.

Weighing promised joys of married life
Against rural poverty –
Added all her grit.

Using every inborn skill to make
Penuary and hard worked patch
Keeps her clad and fed.

Loving, caring,sharing ceaselessly –
Then like wrens the flicker years
Crowd their wedding nests.

Resting on a long life's outer edge,
Sick and deaf and blind, there comes
Faint mouth-corner smiles.

Seeing memory's stirred ash arouse
Rustic, stale-milk Poggios –
Sparks too spent to flame.

1978
Waiting for her to be free at last;
Free of orchids, leopards,snakes
Sweet, sweet immortelle.

Sarah Bath Dunstan – my Grandmother, Poggios – Bread Sops ?

SEA BURIAL

Uncle Tom Dunstan aged 87
Homeward bound from Africa

Below the grey vault of the sky
The cruciform sea gulls are keening.
Gently the swell rocks the cradled ship.
And with long flowing fingers caress it.
A fleeting agitation on the sea's face –
Then it is quickly enfolding.

I BELONG HERE

(Above the Red River near Tuckingmill)

On this tumbled corse,
But barely clothed in tattered cloak
O green and heather red,
The necrophillic chimneys fingers play;
Beyond the stream skulled buildings
Lie broken on their mullocked graves.
In the tree of my blood
A lost memory is sadly singing
Of a maid of the Bal
Who with what anonymous shade
Once laid long, long ago
To bring me to this treeless corruption.

A NUN WITH SCHOOLCHILDREN
MET ON CAMBORNE HILL.

On this lilac-blossomed morning,
Pacific in the turbulence,
The Little Lorelei of Christ
Smiles gently as the shrilling cries
Raise high a spray of urgent wants.
Like white butterflies her hands
Go fluttering from head to head,
To shoulder, or softly alight
On upraised, cherubic faces:
Life's salt enjoyed by virtue
O another woman's act of love.
Her ancient garb is no disguise.
Here is a maiden , nubile, fair.
Who'd grace the common habit
Yet forfeits its days and nights to woo
A Prince – a glittering suit.
Cannot she hear within the cell
The urgent, infant cry of God.

OPEN DAY

(Or, Carl Sandberg against the wall)

SOMEONE has pinned a placard poem on
The classroom wall: see the parents pass
It by like blind men looking at strange sounds.
To her companion one is heard to say –
'Edden the parkee floorin luvly dear ?'

Someone with care has limned it bold in
Copper plate; felt-penned nostalgia.
Outside it looks like rain. '- all thayze cheldern
Teeri' 'round would drive me up the bloomin'
Wall. I'm glad I brought me plastic mac'.

Someone, through Carl, can see those old-time films
And hear again the banjos strum, and see
A golden Mississippi moon
Rise clear above a classroom door.
'My George, he sez thay taych a load of tripe'.

Someone has bathed in golden words and walked
The forests of sweet sounds, and nowhere found
A silver maid nowhere a golden boy,
Nowhere the acoylite, but someone, she -
'- Doan't like pert maids mixed up with full grawed booys'.

TAAMZUN DAAW

(Droawnded et Saay)

I wud strep sunsit frum th' sky,
(Anuther 'ower un dark es nawt t'may)
Jest fur a meat ef yu kud waak by
Frum Lyniss
Up, up frum the' thayvun saay
Taamzum Daaw – My Tamzun Daaw.

I wud ryb th' Melky Waayo' stears
An' strean' thim for a dezy chaen
Ef you kud layve thaay emputoonun tears
En Lyunsis
An' weer flowurs 'bout yr nek agaen
Taamzun Daaw – My Tamzuun Daaw.

I wud ass' th' Devul l taak mey sawl away,
(Thess shill es but ets wauken grave).
R'lays et fur ets etumul 'oludsay
O Lyuniss

Ef en baater feer tu may 'e gave
Taamzun Daaw – My Taamzun Daaw.

I wud ent th' saay weth a lepet shills,
Frum Wulf Rwk to Nantuket Lite,
Ef you ded want tu wed b'nayth th' bills
Uv Lyuniss
But 'tes fur you thaay tawt t'nite
Taamzun Daaw – My Taamzun Daaw.

A DESCANT OF BELLS

(for R.S. Thomas)

They fondle the sweet Israeli oranges;
Press hooked arthritic thumbs
Into the sun-drenched fruits of Sicily.
Among Almeria grapes, sly fingers,
Silk-soft milking,
Pinch the profits: swallow my faith.

Although I paint my market-house with fishes –
Doorposts, lintels, walls and roof,
And 'though chapel gossips have it
I'm Christ's Salesman of the Year.'
They cannot see the sign above my door –
'Adamson'

And while they dawdle, balancing harsh hours
Spent-in a gap of cloud'
Against luscious Californian sugar-melons,
I dream of virgin apples I know will fall
In a sunswept village near the sea.
Where the sleek-muscled M.C. snake
Stood up and called the 'Make and Take'
While up and down, and in and out,
We danced in rhythm to the country rock.

A little stream where a slim Undine rising,
Sun-sheened, opalescent, called ,
'Come, come and give yourself...'
And from a hundred miles or more I thought
I heard a descant
From the bells of Manafon,
Of Eglwys-fach, and Aberdaron.

THE PUBLIC SHELL

(On seeing a picture of the young Edith Sitwell.)

The graven image of a mediaeval
Female

With jet and silver grossly overlaid:
Mere 'Façade':

The public shell that hid the forming pearls
Within its whorls.

Then suddenly, as mists will veil the tors,
The picture blurs;

The image cold-eyed critics feasted – gone.
Here maid alone.

In floralled splendour ,classical, unique,
With high-boned cheek

And slender neck, and wondering eyes that saw
Thornbudflowerhaw.

THE LONESOME BITTERN

(On seeing the ageing American poet, Robert Frost, in a television documentary.)

Here was the lonesome bittern
Whose voice boomed out across
The estuarial wilderness.

Whose probing oftimes raised,
High and flashing bright,
Life from the moiling stream.

Who watched the greedy ships
That plied the busy seas,
Derisive sirens hooting.

Car-bound commuters saw
Him from afar fly low
Above his whispering reeds.

To try their slings, slick lads,
Ill versed in country things,
Slung sharp-edged stones – so wide.

Could ever one forget
His country dignity –
Ever, his cruel shame.

That I should see him tamed
And tethered like a Chinese
Fishing Cormorant.

That has no privacy,
No reedy fastnesses –
A cage its living space.

I watched the ancient, waddling
Bird perform by rote
For grasping fisherman.

He died full ripe of years,
Famed far beyond the reeds,
This wise old country bird.

I pray

    You spake him quiet, Death ,
    You softly called his name,
    And gently stroked him to
    The river's farther shore.

INSOLENCE

Last night I remembered
Clearly,
Before I fell asleep in India,
That little man
Naked –
Excepting the tucked-in dhoti modesty –
Sitting ankles crossed, upon a wooden pallet.
So like the gently Ghandiji that,
Once past the crack-open courtyard door,
I turned back to Kodak him,
Unseen
At his ritual ablutions.

      Back through a quarter-century
      And six thousand miles
      The rhythmic singsong chant
      I clearly heard once more.

Rustle of sloughed snakeskin;
Rattle of dead cacti;
Dry as dust draped village streets
That swallowed the wraithed,
Marauding squadrons;
Iridescent swallowtail in a sound-web
Endless as time: its timelessness
Soothing as an evening raga –
A charcoal burners' flute
In the foothills sighing.

Vessel held aloft
The water
      falling

    falling

        falling.

Brazen sun;
Pariah yelping;
Temple bells;
Beggars' whinging;
Transient squaddie clicking.
I had been there – a minute-
He – a year – a hundred years –
A thousand –

Had not one of Sikander's
In-consequential soldiery,
Like me, stopped there and later wondered
At the insolence of conquest.

THE VOTARISTS

From the Church the fruiting mango trees
White doves fly upward through the evening air;
Transmuted plainsong.
A priest strolls slowly on a moonlit path
Murmuring Maria's to a tropic night.

With a swinging lantern beam and ancient spell
A Chowkidar drives off the evil ones
Who threaten from the darkling mango trees.
Behind the votive flame
A Lingham flickers through out the tropic night.

Chowkidar – an Indian

SAILOR IN SUMMERTIME

The breeze smoothed satin fields
Are full of kissing ears
And golden whisperings;
Confidential honeybees
Fumble in a froth of roses
Collecting sweet tributings;
Doves in shady trees
Interminably intone
Their litanies of love;
And nubile maidens wait,
Timorous – aware
When you are a young man
And summer fills the air.

Through the open door
Drift scents and sounds
Not to be confused
With odorous plastic flowers,
(Donated by the Hospice Friends),
Or the pervasive smell
Of perfumed insect spray;
Of friends and relatives
Full of praise and hope –
Being dutiful.

Proud as Ulysses
The still figure sits
In his appointed chair.
The balding head
Rimed with the hoar of age;
The firm jaw; tanned face;

The square set shoulders –
The strong weathered hands
That gripped the dipping oar;
And pulled the salted seine;
And proudly held the helm;
And pulled on board baskets
From bumboats at Port Said;
And held the pacting gourd
With some South Sea beauty –
Now are motionless.

On the walls about
Hang genuine coloured prints
Of Chagal, Picasso,
A gaudy jigsaw puzzle
Boldly signed by Klee;
A Pender picture
Of Mousehole harbour
Full of maybe boats,
(All donated by the Hospice Friends.)
And boats our silent Ulysses
Can never hope again to see –
For once the strong hand
Pointed a metal fish
That drew a wash of death
Across the sullen seas
How long ago?
How many sightless,
Legless years ago.

MELOPOMENE'S MEN

World War One Poets

Melopomene
Had a battalion rare
The sweetest songs they sang
Were bitter-sweet

Over there, over there

Of 'Demoiselles'
Flirting with the sexton shells;
Blackbird's phantomned' in the petalled air
Of Flander's sleet

Over there, over there

Of those fey men
Who heard the skylark where
It's descent clearly rang
A counter beat

Over there, over there

The choking cloud;
The stifling, slimy shroud;
The silvered Judas flare
Pointing Death's elite

Over there, over there

That life is not
The pleasant and the fair
But a bitter pang
That death complete

Over there, over there

With pencil stub
And grubby page, (their club
and banner), they declare
Life obsolete

Over there, over there

The singers gone
To deaths beyond compare.
The sweetest songs they sang
Were bitter-sweet

Over there, over there

LANDSCAPE WITH THE
FALL OF ICARUS

7.3.5cm x 112cm. Brussels, Musees Royaux des Beaux-Arts

The nor-east breeze eases the burden of the day
The sturdy ploughman sensitively treads
The turned turf – testing the spring-sunned soil.
Time now for sowing.

Undistracted, the fisherman casts out
He knows what life is all about –
Waiting, watching, catching, losing.

> With so little time between
> The Spring and the dying Fall.

At rest upon his staff the shepherd,
Sun upon his back, stands unperturbed –
He knows serving, rearing, killing

> With so little time between
> The Spring and the dying Fall.

To within half a centimetre
The experts have surveyed this landscape
Rod, staff, plough - our certain hereditaments
- Clearly delineated.

RETURN OF THE NIGHTFARER

Weightless
I float again
Over water meadows
Where long horned, dappled kine,
And glistening descendants of the Barb
Still as polished bronzes,
Stand – stand
Over verdant parkland
And bosky woods;
Past pristine places –
Exquisitely proportioned;
Formal gardens
And sylvan avenues
Planned with geometrical precision;
Fountains with spread plumes,
Filigreed screens of water,
Set in silence.
Poplars, three or four,
Never more,
Plyoned across the bright hills,
Are my dark beacons
Denoting the boundary,
Beyond the starless shield,
Whence comes the silvery light.
Silently drift toward
That more fearful toward
That more earful frontier
Beyond the water meadows,
Beyond the dark woods,
Where no shield protects.

Chanticleer tongues his clarion.
Cats cut by queens,
Castaway on reefs of lust,
Loudhail their desolation;
Round about my dreams quadraphonic groupings
Of insomniac mongrels
Mangle Maxwell Davies;
The defiant clock ratchets
Gentle moonlight's one-eyed master
Glaring horizionward;
The nightfarer has returned.

TO THE COMPUTER PROGRAMMER

(SYLVICULTURE)

When my great, great grand-daughter has turned three
Will she take my doddering daughter out to see
Her first, her 'reely' first, computered tree ?
And will her Mother share the child's ecstasy,
Or with inner eye search out a withered memory ?

THEOPHOLOUS

(Descendant of Pashti)

Out tabby, Theo dreams or, so it seems.
His fur ripples like water when a wind
Whisper disturbs a slumberous pool.
Whiskers flicker as some forgotten mouse
Stumbles into a waiting memory cell.
Comfortably contorted he lies, and runs –
One paw marking time upon the air.
Above a paw-wrapped nose, a cold eye
Watchful as history proclaims; I
Theopholous, descendant of the sons
Of Egypt's goddess, Pashti, rightful heir
To worship, condescend to guard this house.
But, ingrate, you accuse a god of dreams,
Neglectful sleep. Show me <u>one</u> mouse, thou fool.

TYGER ? TIGGER ?

She moves among the unseeing
Zombies, Trogs, Walking Dead,
As smoothly as the Lizard Light
Afloat upon its mercury bed.

Always the danger signal –
The little ear that peeps,
Blush pink, from fine-spun amber hair,
To warn of roués, goats or creeps.

My greeting seems to be unheard,
Head down and turned aside.
Then, haughtily , the laser gaze
To raze the satyr in his stride.

The children by her side
Her nights with Paris prove ? –
Temerities of ginger hair,
Poor caricatures of love.

Today upon the café step
We met, face close to face,
Then swiftly, supple animal,
She broke away at quickening pace.

But not before I'd clearly seen,
Raging in the pupil's pool,
A fiercing, luminous, striped beast
Not a mackintoshed old fool.

A GIFT OF POMADE

In imitation of Po-Chu 772-846

An officer brought your gift of pomade
Then marched on towards the Shan' Hills
From where ambitious Chang's soldiers rarely returns;
What needless trouble man's vanity causes.

What need have I for this pomade
Who am old, soon to join Ju-man
At Hsiang-shan where the payer bells ring
Incessantly for every man – even Chang; even me

SOURED SEASON SENRYU

The Festive season
Harassed by children and work
The memory fails.

The unused tablets
Of twentyone memories
So anger my lord.

How implacable
Is my lord's anger over
My forgetfulness.

He threatens he will
Return me to my father:
Forgets my dowry.

My lord dishonours
The mother of his children –
Ogling pretty youths.

At the place they call
'The Inn of the Happy Men'
My lord forgets me.

'IT CAME OFF IN.......'

My daughter Sarah is accident prone
    Her world is an unprotected zone.
    One day she will knock it over the edge
    And be stranded in limbo – alone.